DISABILITY
𝒯𝑜
ABILITY

BY: JA'NIECIA GILMORE

Copyright © 2024 by Seazons Collections Publishing House.

Copyright © 2024 by Scirocca Publication.
Copyright © 2024 by Ja'niecia Gilmore.

All rights reserved. No part of this book may be reproduced or used in any manner without written permission of the copyright owner.

A Message from the Author

"Your strength and resilience shine brighter than any challenge you face. You are capable, valued, and your spirit is truly inspiring. Never let anyone dim your light."

Table of Contents

Chapter 1: From Disability to Ability   1

Chapter 2: Knowing Your Value   4

Chapter 3: Accepting Who You Are   10

Chapter 4: Overcoming Challenges   19

Chapter 5: Walking Into Your Destiny   29

Chapter 6: One Step Away   41

Chapter 1

From Disability to Ability

Sometimes you have to forget what the world label you as and know who God says you are. We get caught up in so many distractions and we lose sight of what God has called us to be on earth. This book is going to explain how I overcame the world and life challenges with having a disability. It also explains how I allowed God to take control over my life and from feeling incapable of doing anything. But then God gave me the ability to fight the odds in what people said and knowing truly what God say. What he says, it never fails.

From Disability to Ability

Going through life with Turner Syndrome was not an easy thing to deal with; and the symptoms that comes with. It's not easy to adjust to one of the symptoms of being short stature and having a genetic disorder that not only affects females, but it causes developmental and health problems. The life expectancy women are slightly shorter than normal. Women can get pregnant, but not naturally. It's very rare. But you can get a donor egg and get pregnant that way. Individuals that has has Turner Syndrome are missing an X chromosome and its missing from most of our cells. That causes a delay in our growth and it has a risk of ovarian failure. It increases obesity in women and other health issues. These are the effects of having Turner Syndrome and the symptoms that comes with every woman that has it.

Having to get through everyday life and knowing how to function with such difficulties and aching, our goal as women is to achieve. So, as you read this book, it's going to take you through my journey and how I was able to get through life and learning how to accept and love who I was created to be.

Chapter 2

Knowing Your Value

Understanding my value was something that I was challenged with because I allowed my value to be determined by the world instead of allowing God to be the author and finisher of my story. No man can take what God gives and what God does. Realize, you can not allow the world to distract you from what God has called you to be. There may be times where you feel inadequate or feel not equipped. But God will always equip you.

No matter if you have a disability, no matter what you have, you are enough. When God created you, it was enough. I used to feel like I was left out. I used to feel like I was different from all of the world; from different people. I used to feel as if I didn't fit in anywhere. Sometimes God doesn't allow you to fit in because he wants you to realize who you are and that you don't have to change for the world, you don't have to change for nobody else. You are wonderfully created in God's image no matter who you are, no matter what you have done or no matter what you may face. God will be with you every step of the way. The times that you mess up, the times that you feel like you don't know who you are, when you don't love yourself or anyone, God is there.

I often said, "You know, I try to fit in with different crowds that didn't fit me and you allow me to be quiet because I felt that who I was wasn't enough." But God will show you that you are enough. God will lead you because you are special to God and that is something I had to learn. I am special in God's eyes, even when the world doesn't see it. You can't be too hard on yourself when you mess up. You can't be too hard on yourself because you may not know certain things or you may not understand certain things. It's ok to not know everything. As long as you keep going, as you keep pursuing and pushing towards your mark, pushing towards your goals, pushing towards what God has called you to be, and not lowering your value for anyone else. Only God knows who you are. People don't know who you are or what you are capable of doing. Don't allow the world and its critics limit you. Don't allow anything to limit who you are. For example: as I enter school and need assistance in certain accommodations, that many people didn't need. But for me specifically, I needed that because they help me to pass. It helps me to understand the material that I was learning. I kind of felt embarrassed that people didn't need help, but I did. Then I learned that this was something that was beneficial for me and it's something that most people need.

Sometimes it's ok to ask for help. It's ok to not understand things. Don't feel ashamed that you don't understand. Continue through school. I didn't really have much friends that understood me or that I could relate to. It was kind of difficult for me to make friends. But what I learned is, sometimes if you don't fit in with certain people, it's ok because the person that God has for you, will come. You will know that they were sent by God.

I was bullied throughout Elementary and Middle school because I didn't fit in. I didn't look like certain people and I didn't talk like them. I was very sheltered as a kid because I allowed my disability to limit who I was. That doesn't take away for who you are inside. There is something beautiful beyond what the world see and beyond what the natural eyes can see. One thing I know is what God sees, how he looks at us and how he views us. He didn't create nothing on purpose, nor accident. It's all predestined. He predestined us for greatness. He has created us to his likeness. Not how the world should like us. No man can change the destiny that God has for you. It is set in stone. Despite of all the odds that she may face, in spite of all the trauma, in spite of her pain and rejection, there is greatness beyond the surface. God did not give into the world's standard of what beauty is, or what you should look like, or what you're capable of. I want us to go forth and God wants us to persevere. He doesn't want us to be worried or doubtful of anything. He wants us to keep our eyes on him. When you keep your eyes on him, you can't focus on how you feel or what's around you. God is bigger than all of the problems that you may face. When you feel like you can't go on or when you feel like you can't endure, God will give you the strength to persevere. Your worth is so much more to God than this world. God has a purpose for you. There's nothing he has done by accident.

The world will always fail you, but God would never fail you; even when you feel like you cannot go on. When I felt alone, when I felt like the world was against me, I know someone who was with me and I was God. "If God is for me, who can be against me?"

You have so much more work to do on this

earth. You cannot quit. You cannot give up. You cannot allow how you feel determine who you are. No matter what you may be facing, there's so much more to your story than your disability. It wasn't sent to break you, it was sent to make you. It was sent to build you and transform you into the person you are today.

God knows your story before you do. God knows the ending and he knows the beginning. So trust him and never change your value for no one else. Your value is with God, not the world. You are more precious than rubies and gold. Instead of looking, how the world perceives you, focus on how God sees you. In his eyes, he created a masterpiece. He created no mistakes. He didn't create you to be in the world, he created you to be separate from the world. He said, "Be separate, for I am separably Holy. For I am Holy." In holiness it takes sacrifices but it's worth it at the end.

Chapter 3

Accepting Who You Are

There's no one that can do what you do. There's no one that can speak how you speak, talk how you talk, or walk how you walk. There's only one of you. So cherish who you are and love who you are. Don't devalue yourself. Love how God created you because no one can fulfill the destiny that God has for you expect you. As for me, it took a while for me to accept just how God created me. I didn't understand why I have to endure so much pain and so much judgment in the world because of my disability. I always wanted to hide. I really didn't want to go anywhere. I didn't know how to express myself. I didn't know how to talk. I didn't know how to live life. Not knowing that I was isolating myself and that I was allowing myself to be in a place that wasn't for me. I was comparing myself with people instead of allowing God to fulfill all of those voids that I was trying to fill with the world.

It's not easy living with a disability. Some days you may feel lost. Then some days you may feel empty. Some days you may even feel unworthy. Most days you just don't want to go on. For a long time I was putting on a mask, hiding who I was and who God created me to be. I was very sheltered. I was shy. I wasn't outspoken as other people was because I thought that my voice didn't matter or that who I was, didn't matter. But when I found God, that's when I found myself.

When I started to love myself, that's when I started to understand who I was. God will create something imperfect and transform it to the perfect piece for him. He can make something out of nothing. All of those challenges that I was going through, was only to push me into my destiny. When I gave my life to God, it was the best choice I could've ever made because that's when I became free. That's when I started to understand who I was and who he was. I started to listen to God's words and not the world. Declining every negative voice and began listening to what he says because my God doesn't lie. If he said it, he would do it. If he did it before, he would do it again. He's the same God then and he's the same God now. He never changes his word. He stands on his every promise that he has given to you. He will fulfill it and that's when I knew that I was special in his eyes. I said I was his child and that he cared for me enough to show me. He pulled me from doubt, shame, pain and hurt. He gave me victory over my story! Victory over my life! He declared that I have victory in every area of my life.

The feet is natural portion. You don't have to take in what the world says. When you withhold the world's opinions, you allow those things to be in you. God never wanted us to carry the world. I realize when I try to carry over my problems and pain, I was carrying a burden of the world. God didn't want me to carry the weight of the world. He wanted me to cast my cares on him and know that he will fulfill my every need and desire. He will put into place everything in his timing. He loves you. He knows you are enough. If you can see how God sees you, that's enough. He knows every plan he has for you. Plans to prosper you. He gives you hope in the future so don't despise the journey that God has given you. God has already prepared your journey. Good it's going to come out of your story. God will get the glory out of your story. His love will shine in you and through you. So don't quit the process because the process is necessary. The journey is necessary. It's necessary for you to get through this journey. You won't be like everyone else. You can't be like everyone else. You are who God created you to be. Can't no one be who you are. Can't no one walk in your shoes. You don't have to answer to no one. You don't have to please anyone except God.

You don't have to devalue yourself for no one. You don't have to think less of yourself because he has your life in the palm of his hands. You just have to trust him with it.

Sometimes it's hard to accept who you are when you have so many people that are coming against you, telling you all these things that God never said you were. It's hard to love who you are. It's hard to not allow the world opinions to control how you feel about yourself. But one thing I have to realize is that man will fail you. But God will never fail you. God has put everything in order how he wanted it to be.

Growing up with my disability, I had a depression disorder. Several thoughts of loneliness and isolation because I was so worried of what people would think or what people would say. I felt that I wasn't enough. I allowed myself to be in a dark space and allowed the enemy to plant seeds in me to where I believe that, instead of believing what God says. Regardless of your thoughts that you have, you can allow it to manifest and to grow into something big or you could capture it before it takes place. The spirit of loneliness and depression, is not God. We are allowed to grow from those spirits and be bigger than that. We are bigger than our thoughts. When we think of what he says about us, and what he has promised us, we are bigger. Our natural is what we will focus on above all.

What did god say about you? Who did God say you are? Those are the questions that you need to ask yourself because when you get those answers, you will be complete. Because of God, you are complete. In him, you will live. In him, you are healed. In him, you are delivered. In him, you are set free. You're no longer in bondage because of the world. I was in bondage. But because of God, I was free from hurt, from the harsh words people would say, from the bullying, free from lying and feeling unworthy. All those things canceled out when I found Jesus. All of the silent battles that I had to go through, he was there. He would never leave you or forsake you. He was there for me because what he did for me, he can do the same for you. No matter what physical thing you may be dealing with. God look at the heart because he knows our desires. He knows our intentions and that's all that matters. To be right in his eyes, not right in the world's eyes. Not trying to please the world and not trying to fit in. He has called us to be separate.

Those times where I was like an inconvenience in this world or where I felt like I was the problem in peoples eyes, when I wasn't. Not knowing that God called me to be extraordinary in my own way. I wasn't a problem. It was that the world had a problem with me. I didn't have the problem with the world. Sometimes you may face times in your life where you are battling God. Asking which direction should you take because one of the directions pulling you the other way and it's like you are in between. It feels like you don't know which way to go. You feel lost when you want to follow God. But then another part of you want to help, love, and be there for people when they was never there for you.

But because God's mercy, you don't have to do

much for him to come to your rescue. No matter the mistakes, no matter what you have done, no matter who you are, God can make something that looks dirty, become clean. He's the one that can clean you up. He's the one that can purify you. He's the one that can improve everything in you that the world can't do. God is man that he doesn't lie. When he says he will do it, trust him.

Keep in mind, you have something special that nobody else have. Nobody's perfect. I made so many mistakes. But when I tell you he will use someone broken and he will put you together. You will come out brand new. You still may not get everything right, but that's the process that you have to go through that you can't skip and that you can't deny. You are a work in progress. In God's will, the work that you do, can't nobody else do. If you allow him to be who he is.

Do you know him? Do you know that he loves you? From the situations and places that broke you, he can build you back up. Once he builds you, you can't go back. Once you are in with God, you have no choice but to change. You can't stay the same. When I tried to stay in my mess that I was in, things didn't work out well. I was comfortable. God don't like you to be comfortable. He wants you to flourish. He wants you to grow in him. I went knowing that I had a disability. I was blinded. When I came to God, God took the shield off of my eyes, and he allowed me to see who I was.

As a child I never knew why I had deal with so much pain, so much turmoil, so much rejection, abuse physically, mentally and spiritually too. But that was because I was chosen. When you are chosen, you experience things that may seem too much to bear. But God already has you equipped. I didn't want to go to those battles but he already knew what I would get through so he could get the glory out of my story.

Chapter 4

Overcoming Challenges

The part that no one wants to talk about. The challenging parts of coping with disabilities. There's so many obstacles that we face in life. Because I had Turner Syndrome, in school it affected me, it affected my health, it affected my confidence and also my friendships. While on school, I had to receive help. I had to have certain accommodations. Most people didn't want to help because of my disability. I felt awkward getting help, thinking all these things. Then I realize that it was ok for me to receive help. But I allowed my feelings and myself to get in the way of embracing who I was, embracing help, and embracing things that I needed. Not knowing, it was ok for me to get those things. But I didn't realize that. It was hard for me to understand certain things in class. It was hard for me to understand certain material, so I had to study hard and push harder. I became frustrated because I didn't know why I couldn't do things as fast as others did. But then I realize that some people learn easier than others. I had to strive harder while in school every day trying to get my education. I really didn't have friends because people just don't understand me. Some people understood me and some people I met were only around for a season and a reason. But always remember, it's ok. People can't go with you where God is taking you. Nonetheless, I made the best out of it. I made the best out of my situation. That's when I start to get closer to God.

In spite of all the obstacles, all the battles, all of the unheard cries that I did at night, despite the frustration, in spite of the doubt, despite of the worrying, God restored all of that and he allowed me to see that I can do anything I put my mind to. All things are possible! When you add him in every part of your life, you will succeed. As I did that, I graduated high school. I walked on a stage and I got my diploma, proud with my head held high knowing that God did that for me.

When God does something, you would know with him. You would know that he is who he is and that he is a promise keeper. You will know that he is a redeemer and that he's there all of the time.

So count it all joy when you have obstacles in life. That doesn't mean that your story has come to an end, it means God has something better for you on the other side. He will lead you to the witness it and he will lead you to the promised land. But you have to stay on the course. You have to stay on track. You cannot give up in the middle of the race. You can't give up in the middle of the journey. If I would've gave up in the middle of my journey, I wouldn't have graduated. But because I trusted him and I decided to put my own feelings to side, I gained his favor.

God is evident. When you become detailed with God, he will give you everything you ask for. God hears our prayers and he will take all of that and create it into something beautiful. God will hold your hand every step of the way. He will not let you fall because if he started it with you, he will finish with you. Our job is to not look back, but look forward. To not let circumstances to make you but allow your circumstances to change you for the better.

Even as I am still continuing in college now, that really encourage me to know that if I can get through high school, I can get to college with him by my side. It's nothing that he will not do for you because we are over-comers. We are more than conquerors in Christ Jesus. We are victorious. We will never be defeated. See the devil will make you feel that you are defeated, only to realize that God made you victorious in him.

Every thing that you need in this life you don't have to worry because everything you need is inside of you. You are the greatest gift to anyone in the world. You are the prize in anyone that sees it. They will not miss handle you. They will not misuse who you are. He will make all your places straight. He lets you rest in green meadows and he leads you beside peaceful streams. Meaning that he would give us peace in the mist of of all the storms and battles. The challenges that you are facing in this life, he will allow you to rest and give you joy in the midst of the storm.

There were times where I was battling with my disability and going through all of these emotions. When I want to hang out with friends or go have sleepovers, I would have to take my medicine with me. Then when I took my medicine with me, my friends will see me take a shot in my leg and at times I felt embarrassed because I hate them to see me that way or see me taking this medicine. I felt different. I feel like an outcast because I was taking this medicine and they didn't have to. I will have to take a shot in my leg at night because I usually take it at home. But when I have to travel places, I will have to take it with me in order to get my medication. It was like extra weight that I was bringing with me that I didn't feel comfortable bringing. I would get so tired of taking my medicine. I would get drained and I would want to stop. But I knew that I had needed it so I can get the benefits of my medicine. Which was to help me to grow as tall as I can. Girls with Turner Syndrome, they don't grow as tall as normal girls. So, I needed that medicine to help me grow even more.

I disliked going to the doctor because I knew that they were going to say something that maybe I didn't like. I dreaded going to the doctor because of my disability and honestly I was scared. Not of the doctor, but the results. But I didn't know that it was a God that would change the results of the doctor and change it to what he said in his words. HEALED!

When I looked at the scripture, I started to realize that this is only temporary. God knows the beginning to the end. That's when I finally accepted who I was, what I had, and the things that I had to do. I wasn't afraid andI wasn't worried anymore because then I found peace within myself. My disability doesn't count me out, but it makes me count on God.

Why live afraid? Why live hidden when God never told us to be hidden. He told us to be unique because we were wonderfully made in his image. So if he created us to be one-of-a-kind, we are his masterpiece. There's nothing missing nothing or lacking in us because he dwells in us.

Allow God to take full control in your life. Fully submit everything to him because when you are open to him, he's open to you. He's all around you. There's nothing you cannot hide from him. So why hide from him? All he wants is your heart and to be open to him. His love never ends. His love never fails and his love for us is never ending. His love never runs dry. He loves you enough to pick you up out of a place that was dry and put you up in a place that was filled with over flow of with milk and honey. But we have to want it.

Don't worry about how you may look, how you

may sound or what you don't have. Love him for who he is. Love him in the present time. He's bigger than anything you can think of. He will follow us to the end of the earth. So when you feel like life is too hard to live, he will give you the strength to go forth. You are created for a purpose and for a reason. Do not dread on what he has created you with, and how he created you. He will never hurt us. He will protect us. So we have to give our thoughts to him. Everything that we have been afraid of, give to him and be honest. That's all he wants is a relationship with you because he loves you. He's concerned about you. So live life because you never know when God will come. We're only here once. So live life to the fullest. Live in his will that's pleasing to him. Not in the world.

I have a allowed myself to be content in him. Everything else around me is content. Allow God's love to pour out on you. Just receive him. That's the best thing you can do. It was the best decision I ever made. It made life worth living. He gave me life to breathe again and he never look at my mistake or the things I said. He looks at the heart and he see that my heart was open to him. All that matters is that you believe who he is and that he will heal every pain that you may have felt. He feel exactly how you feel. He understands what happened and how we feel sometimes.

Life can take a toll on you, drain you and make give you feel defeated. But he gives us victory over everything in our lives. Enjoy the moment and seek him. When I found him, that's when he drew close to me, and he revealed himself even more to me. It's not that we are far away, he just wants us to come to him, but he's right there. He's always been right there. He's the one that will clean and make us brand new. He made me brand new. He turned my story into victory. He will give you victory out of your life and out of your story today. Nothing that happened in your life was a mistake but for a purpose. He would never go back on his word. Every promise that he has promised you, you will reap them. Focus on what he said, and not on the world and what they say. Accept that we can't change what happened in our lives but we can look ahead and move forward. What God has for us press towards the mark of the high calling because there is a purpose there for you.

Chapter 5

Walking Into Your Destiny

Think about walking into your destiny. First, you have to know who you are. You have to first accept your destiny that God has for you. You have to acknowledge that the destiny God has for you is enough. Don't look at other people journey and destiny. Don't doubt your destiny because the destiny God has for you, is for you. He put it right in the right place. He made you in the right place. He made everything about you right.

In order to love who you are, you have to first fine who you are in God. When you find who you are in God, that's when you find your destiny. When you don't find who you are, you walk in turmoil in this world. But when we find out what God wants for us, we become untouchable. But when we walk into the opposite direction of what God has planned for us, we become attack by the world.

Walking towards your destiny sometimes can look uncomfortable, but you have to know that God has given you all the tools that you need for the destiny for the journey. He has led you to the journey. He will not leave you in the middle of the journey, no matter how hard it may seem. Sometimes we can look at our own problems and we can look at our own selves and we can't forget the destiny God has for us. For me, dealing with my disability and not knowing who I was, was challenging.

God will direct me in my destiny. We can go in our own ways and we could do the opposite thin. Sometimes we get distracted from the opposite direction that we are going in. But God has not made any mistakes. When I was dealing with my disability, I was confused. I was the loss. I was walking in a path that was in darkness. I got so angry at myself that I thought that I didn't have no purpose in this life because of my disability. All because of what people claim as a disability when it's when it's not a disability. God could do all things because he created me. And if I follow him, I can do all things through him. He has given me the ability to walk, to speak, and do everything I desire. He will grant you all the desires of your heart if you seek him first. The Kingdom above all else and above all things. He wish that you would be in good health, just as your soul prospers. He wants you to be in right standings with him. The destiny that he has for you, no man in the world cannot change the destiny that he has for you. It is already set in stone. So we have to embrace the destiny.

Sometimes we have our own plans when God has so much more for us. Sometimes we can limit our own self. You can even limit God. We'll try to put our own destiny in front of us without allowing

God to put his destiny in front of us. His destiny will lead us in the right direction. His destiny will lead us in the right path. As we continue to walk with him, he will continue to abide in us. So with revealing who I was, and seeking God even more, you know, I'm not allowing my disability to make me. But to allow it to make me be a overcomer because the world labels you. But it doesn't matter what the world says. As long as you speak, you seek, and hear what he says, his word will not turn to you void. Whatever you say, he will do whatever he promises. He will finish what he started. He will not leave you in the middle of this journey no matter how hard it may be. He loves us too much to leave us. It don't matter what you have, who you are, what color you are, how you were raised, how tall you are, your weight or your disability, none of that defines who you are. You are more than enough! Don't look at what you see now because there's so much more that he has planned for us. He has plans to prosper us and to give us a hope in the future. So stand in the promises of God and what he has called you to do. Stand in what he has created you to do. God loves every part of you. From flaws and all of the mistakes. All of that is for his glory and for his purpose. Yes, you might mess up in the middle of journey! Yes, you might stumble and fall but you have to get back up. It may be some hills and valleys but he will never let you fall. No matter which way you go, he's right there always.

Sometimes our destiny may be different from God's plans for us. Sometimes we can choose our plans and it may not align with God's plan. We had to line up with God's plans and what he wants. As you seek him, he will give you the desires of your heart. It's more than just a destiny. It's the path that he has created you with to live in righteousness and holiness. Free from all things. That's the path that he wants you to go on. The straight and narrow path because there's so much more than you even know that he has for you. You just have to give him your all because if you resist him, you will limit the things that he wants to do in your life. No one can walk in the destiny that God specifically designed for you only because he has equipped you. He has allowed you to walk the destiny that he has for you because he knew that you can get through it. He knew that you were qualified to do it. The world may disqualify us and you may feel disqualified in areas of your life, but God qualifies. He says you're qualified.

So when you feel like you have no place on this earth, when you feel like there's no other way to go, when you feel like nothing is normal, remember if God is for you, who can be against you! When things seem like they are coming against you, you have the one and only God that's for you. He has everything you. He has put everything in your hands that you need. You just have to look within and unlock it. Seek and you will find. Knock, and the door shall open. Don't resist him, don't deny the destiny he has for you and don't delay the destiny. He asked for you to follow him. Many are chosen. He will not lead you astray. You are capable to do everything you put your mind to. You were designed for greatness. You are meant to be victorious, to conquer, to defeat all that come against you in this life. You will not be defeated. You rise above everything. You will prevail. You will succeed. You are meant to soar like eagles. You are the head and not the tail. You are the lender and not the borrower. God will provide all your needs according to his riches and glory. Many challenges you may come against, some barriers, your back may be against the walls, but God will tear down every barrier just like he did the wall of Jericho.

You are his masterpiece. Our gift that God has given us, is already within us. All we have to do is activate it. It's already in you. You have a destiny inside of you that you can't afford to sleep on, and that you can't afford to abandon. So don't look as if you can't do it because he will give you the strength to do it. Don't allow fear to make you captive but be free. He wants you to be free. He wants you to just live a life that is abundant because I think I realize it's not how you do it, it's how you go through it. It's not how fast you get there, it's the journey in the middle of the test that matters. It's how you get through it. It's how you handle the situation. If you keep your faith in all circumstances, even when they look like impossible, God will turn it possible. Nothing is impossible with God. The promises that he has for you, he hasn't forgotten you. Everything will come at the right time and everything will come to pass. You will see the goodness of the lord in the land of the living. You will see how the Lord is good. You will see how the Lord is faithful. So sand tall like a Mecca tree that's planted. Stand firm so when things come, it cannot reroute you or distract you from what he has for you.

Lean on him as you walk with him. You don't have to worry about the things that surround you because he will handle all that. At some point, I felt like I had to do everything and I had to be the one to control. But when you are released, you give that control to God and you get yourself out the way. He's not going to come into your life when you are feeling like you have control because we cannot do anything on our own strength, but his strength.

With his grace and with his power, we can do all things. His will is perfect. His way is perfect. So don't look to the left and don't look to the right. Keep your eyes focused straight ahead towards the mark of the high calling.

Destiny is not just for you, but it's for generations to come. You can do all things, but fail. You will not lose this battle. You won't lose. You will never fail because he will never fail you. He will break every generational curse. He will break everything that is meant for evil, and he will turn it for your good. He wants the wall that you have build up and he wants you to be vulnerable with him and tell him everything. Don't hold back nothing from him. Just say, "Here I am". He's right there because he knows what you want. He knows what you need, where you are and where you should go. He has designated you to be the person he created. Not angry, not depressed, not sad, not to worry and not the doubtful person. Those things are nothing but the enemy. He has created you to live life abundantly. Have joy, have peace and have a sound mind. You have to be very careful who you give access to. Sometimes we give access to the enemy. But it's your choice to give in or walk past those odds in and defeat. He gives us choices. That's the good thing about God, that he gives a choice. If he gives us the option, he doesn't restrict us nor make us do anything. He wants nothing but the best for us. We can't follow the world's way. It's his way or no way. We have to be available for God.

All of those dark days all of those days where you feel that God is silent, he's listening to you. He's just waiting for you to be receptive to his voice, because he's always listening to you. Now you just have to be in a place where you listen to him and he will give you destruction to tools that you need in the journey. The race is not given to the swift nor the humble but those who do endure to him. If you walk by faith, then what you see don't matter because everything that you see is just temporary. You have to have faith, believe and know that he is and will be there for you. Everything he has started in your life, he will finish. He will fill your life with nothing but the good things. All you need is him. He is the one that can regulate your mind. He is the one that can speak things into your life. He is the one that can open doors. He is the one that can close doors. He's the one that will give access to the things that you need. He is the Alpha and Omega. So all you have to do is know that he is everything that you need. Nothing or no one can satisfy what you need or your soul, but God. The flesh is weak. So the flesh only wants nothing but evil. But the spirit loans for righteousness. When people see your destiny and the walk that you are walking, then it will allow people to follow and want to know more of God. But you have to be in a place that is obedient. He wants you to be obedient. He wants you to be with me. He wants a willing vessel. That's all he wants. Yes, all he wants to know is that if he can count on you to do the things you say. When it all said and done, we will have to give account to him and the only words that I want to hear and we shall hear is, "Good and faithful servant, you have done a good job."

When you have a relationship with him, he would give you peace. You will not be led astray. The Holy Spirit will guide you and will not lead you astray. God didn't just die for us to have no direction or to be lost. He wants us to really know who he is and what we are worth to him. Not the worth the world portrays him to be. That's when you will know your destiny.

Chapter 6

One Step Away

Sometimes we could be one step away from walking into our purpose. We could be one step away from walking into what God has for us. Sometimes we can be so focus on what the world say and what people say. We get so distracted and we can miss what God wanted to do in our lives. But what we had to know is that God knows our steps. He said the steps of a righteous are ordered. So he orders our steps. He prepares a table before us so he has everything in order and writes it in place. But we have to get in alignment with him. As we are out of alignment, we can never walk into our purpose because that means that we are out of alignment.

Don't miss what God is doing. It was one part of my life where I used to doubt God's plans. I used to doubt who God called me to be. I used to be afraid. I used to deny who God called me to be. Not knowing that all God wanted for me was just to take the leap into my destiny. Sometimes we have to believe who God called us to be and trust that he know everything. As long as we walk with him daily and have faith in him, he will never fails us. One reason why we have to take one step is because if we look back, we will never walk into the purpose that God has for us. If we look back on what we could've fixed, what happened or what didn't work out, we were never walking to the purpose that God has. Yes, we all have things that we have to conquer. Yes, we all have things that we have to face. But as long as we look forward and look above, you keep pushing forward to the mark of the high calling. That's all God wants for us. If we trust him and give him our all, he will give us his presence. We have to stop rejecting the love that God wants to give us because his love is unconditional. His love is never ending. He makes no mistakes.

He made no mistakes when he made us. We are all designed for a reason, for a purpose and for a season. We are precious in God's eyes. So every step that you take, every breath that you take, he's with us. Every heartbeat we have, that's his life dwelling in us. He gave us his life when died to sin and bondage. God reversed everything that was meant for evil, and he turned it around for a good. So he gave us life instead. He gave us purpose because everything that we go through is for a purpose. Everything that we have gone through, we have conquered is for a purpose and for a reason. He is forever faithful and we are his treasure. He loves us and he's concerned about everyone.

He is concerned about the things that upsets us. He's concerned about the things that we cannot speak about. As long as we are honest with him, that is us taking a leap of faith and taking one step. All god wants is us to be honest with him. He gave us a choice to get it right. As long as we are on this earth, we have a chance to do it right and to give him our all. Sometimes the things that we go through, it's not to get us down. But everything that we go through is for God to get the glory out of our lives.

In order for God to get his purpose in our lives, sometimes we have to release our will, our wants, all of the desires and yield them over to God. We must allow him to do the perfect work. Sometimes we don't realize how much we are holding on to the weight that we carry. It's not for us to carry. It's for God. We so worried about the weight instead of waiting on God. At times, things may seem very difficult and they feel as if you cannot get through it. Sometimes you may even feel like you aren't qualified to do things. But God always qualifies for unqualified.

Sometimes we may want to fall out of the race. But if we just keep pushing, God will push us. You're only one step away from your destiny, from the promise that he has for us. What he promises, he will never fail. It will come to pass as long as we fight through it. As long as we push through every obstacle. Everything that God has put inside of us, he has equipped us to get through it. He will lead us to peaceful streams. He will give us peace in the middle of the journey. Every step that you take, he's with you. He is holding your hand in the middle of your battles. So we can't count ourselves out because we are more than conquerors in Christ Jesus. He will never leave us.

At times it may seem we are defeated. But we are never defeated, we are victorious. We are more than what the world called us to be, what the world has said we are. We are not what people say we are. We are not mistakes. All that matters is what God says. All that matters is if you believe what God says. God said his word will not return to you void. You have to run to him in your weakness. When you lay everything down, he will give you the push you need. He will give you the steps you need to continue on this journey because you have everything you need inside of you. You just have to unlock it. You have to believe that what God has put inside of you, it is not necessary for the other person. It's not a mistake that you are on this earth to just do anything. You have a purpose. You have a destiny. You have a colony that God has put inside of you. There's no one like you. There's no one that can do what you do. There's no one that can fulfill the destiny that God has for you, but you. No one can give what God has put in you. Despite how you feel, despite what you have been through. We have to endure things just like God had to endure things. But the goodness of enduring is that when you can do it, or you will see the good in the land of the living. As long as you continue to endure, prevail and push towards the mark that God has for you, you will win. You have to continue to not look back because you look back, you will be hindered. You will be stagnant in the past. What we left behind, has no purpose for us. But if you look at what is ahead of you, then you will see God's Grace. It is vital.

When he made you, he made you in the likeness of his image. So if you keep going and you walk and not faint, and not get weary, God will take you higher. Your enemies cannot reach you. You will flourish in the things of God. Your life is not a mistake. You cannot afford to give up. From your brokenness, God can make a masterpiece, refine you and transform you. Your destiny has not ended because of your disability but it is just getting started. There's so much you have to offer the world. So keep going. Never be defeated because with God, you can conquer anything the world has thrown your way.

Made in the USA
Columbia, SC
11 December 2024